Suffering Katrina

To order additional copies, please contact us.
BookSurge, LLC
www.booksurge.com
I-866-308-6235
orders@booksurge.com

Suffering Katrina

Personal Stories From Hurricane Katrina's Survivors

T. L. Vidrine

2005

Suffering Katrina

TABLE OF CONTENTS

ACKNOWLEDGEMENTS

Special thanks to my closest friends, Rhonda Laiche who introduced me to most of the survivors, and Juanita Fenley and Debra Vizinat who encouraged me to fulfill my dream. I also thank my family, Greg, Matthew, Maria, and Mitchell, for sacrificing their hours with me during the duration of this project. Most of all, I thank my number one agent, God, who inspired me to help others by using my talents.

This book is dedicated to all the suffering victims of Katrina in Louisiana, Mississippi, and Alabama. May they persevere through it all.

PREFACE

After volunteering to assist the victims of Katrina by collecting and delivering items, I was prompted to visit the shelter to collect personal accounts of events in the lives of the victims so the world could read about the true accounts of these events and also to allow others to see that even though much suffering exists that there is also hope. It is through suffering that we are purified.

I discovered that many wanted to share their stories. Their sharing was a decontamination of their souls.

As you read through these events in the lives of six individuals, remember that what you have heard and seen on television is not always the absolute truth. This book reveals the truth and the hope of the victims and rescue workers in the midst of turmoil.

In our lives, we will be faced with many storms in the form of sickness, nature, and life, but we can overcome the struggles if we place our hope and trust in our supreme being and rely on our neighbors, for without one another and God, we are nothing but an empty body without a soul.

CHAPTER I

Before the Storm

As the sun rose over the eastern horizon of New Orleans, the early morning ringing of the streetcars filled the city to warn commuters that the cars were running and had right of way. Upon hearing the alarms of the street sirens, cars, and tooting taxies, many of the city's vital workforce- cooks, hotel hops, clerks, waitresses, and artists — rose from their slumber as they prepared to hitch a ride to their places of employment.

The aroma of fresh coffee, baked bread, and the wet, dirty streets pervaded the air as a light breeze ran through the city. The stale reek of the French Quarter bars escaped through opened doors while bartenders prepared for a new day of visitors 24/7. The city's night-lights faded into the new dawn of a fresh day in New Orleans.

Slowly, the regular patrons of cafés and family restaurants sipped their coffee and debated whether Hurricane Katrina, hovering in the Gulf of Mexico, would visit New Orleans. The talk of the day was about Katrina, the largest hurricane ever, and if it came to New Orleans, how the bowl shaped city would fill with water because it is under sea level and surrounded by an insufficient levee system. The pseudo engineers each gave their expertise on how the system could be repaired, and the debate of years was once again revisited as Katrina threatened the residents of Louisiana.

In many homes, similar conversations were overheard, and

eyes were pinned to the local television stations waiting for the latest predictions on the path of the storm. School children waited anxiously to hear if they would attend school on Monday morning. Some predicted that the storm would go more easterly of New Orleans and hit Mobile, Alabama because of a front coming into the state, but the low in the eastern part of the United States made this prediction uncertain.

Two days before Katrina made landfall on Saturday, August 27th, most residents of the coastal regions were unclear about the actual path of the storm, but as they waited they prepared as before with other storms. The predicted landfall was early Monday, August 29th. By mid Saturday morning, most old-timers who remembered the devastation of past storms, Betsy and Camille, began evacuations. No mandatory evacuation was ordered early that day, and so this was the view of New Orleans as she prepared two days before the storm.

As the predictions became clearer that New Orleans might be directly hit when the National Hurricane Center issued an updated hurricane advisory for the southeast coast of Louisiana to the Intercostals city to Alabama/Florida border, including New Orleans and Lake Pontchartrain, more residents decided to evacuate later that day. It was then that Governor Kathleen Blanco ordered a mandatory evacuation, and residents hustled to escape from Orleans, St. Bernard, St. Tammany, and other low lying areas.

Thousands of residents from the coastal parishes evacuated from the areas predicted to be devastated by the massive hurricane's wind and rain. While these thousands tried to use the same access for evacuation, the highways and interstate systems filled quickly with stalled, creeping traffic, and it appeared that no one was getting anywhere fast enough. It took hours to get from Kenner to La Place where on a regular day it would have taken only minutes. Upon seeing this problem and predicting that most evacuees would be stranded while trying to evacuate, the Governor ordered a contraflow of traffic. Contraflow began at 4 pm Saturday, and traffic was reversed on the inbound inter-states so that traffic would move quickly out of the city, but still this wasn't quick enough for some, and most would be frustrated as they rolled slowly through parishes to avoid the storm.

Meanwhile, the Red Cross prepared shelters throughout the state for the evacuees, and many fled to them as they drove into areas of uncertainty and waited for the wrath of Katrina while some less fortunate souls, who had no means for evacuating New Orleans, rushed to the Superdome, and others chose to weather the storm in the privacy of their homes. Little did they know, thousands of others chose to do the same. With little provisions for a few days and no means of transportation, these hopelessly trapped residents waited apprehensively for the coming of the storm. Each person had his own reason for staying and the consequences cost him his home, sanity, and life.

In the surrounding parishes, the story was similar. Those evacuating were still seeking shelter as the storm crept closer to the shores of Louisiana. Desperate, some traveled from shelter to shelter where they were turned away as each filled to capacity. Others, in despair, weathered the storm in their vehicles along the highway or in parking lots of shelters further north of Orleans, St. Bernard, and St. Tammany Parishes. A few lucky ones finally found refuge sixty miles outside of New Orleans in an unfamiliar surrounding called Lamar Dixon in Gonzales, Louisiana after hearing about it on the radio.

These shelterless residents sought safety in the safe haven of Lamar after many hours of being rejected. They rode out the storm there, not knowing that soon their place would be filled with more residents of displaced evacuees from the same parishes who were evacuated after the storm, and later they discovered that this place of refuge would become their residence for some time.

As I prepared for the storm, the night before, I accessed the Internet to get a satellite chart of the storm. What amazed me about it were not only the velocity of the winds but also the size and shape. It resembled a huge snake, slowly slithering its way across the vast expansion of the coastal regions.

CHAPTER 2

The Arrival of Katrina

On August 29, 2005, some time after mid morning, Hurricane Katrina, a Category 4, set her eye on arriving in St. Bernard, Louisiana. The category four hurricane force winds pounded the area for hours before finally moving further ashore. Some of the feeder bands extended further into the state with winds measuring up to eighty miles per hour, and some gusts were stronger. While many residents braced themselves that day, Katrina tangoed across the southeastern portion of Louisiana and her neighboring states, Mississippi and Alabama.

As the storm pounded the city with excessive winds, a storm surge of twelve to fifteen feet stressed the city's levee system and surrounding parishes' waterways. (Gyan and Millhollon) It seemed as if New Orleans had weathered the worst of the storm until the levee systems on 17th Street Canal and the 9th Ward gave way to flooding 80% of the city. Rising waters and a weakened levee stressed the 17th street canal levee system, but the 9th Ward system was broken by a barge that rammed into the side of the levee thereby forcing the system to give way.

Water began to rise quickly as levees breached. Unprepared for the massive flooding, the Army Corps of Engineers' relief efforts seemed to wash away with the waters of Lake Pontchartrain and the mighty Mississippi. The suffocating rising waters awakened the unsuspecting, slumbering residents in the 9th Ward and 17th Street Canal, and they had little time to get to higher ground. The water rose so quickly that residents who chose to stay had no warning. In one hour, water rose as high as ten feet.

Fearful, many New Orleanians began to wade their way through chest deep water heading toward the only known safe haven in the city, the Superdome. No one could have predicted what would happen next in the chaotic turmoil of the city's main shelter, or that thousands who didn't evacuate would flock to a new makeshift shelter in the Convention Center.

As flooded victims gathered at the Convention Center, the occupants began to overflow the walkways. Authorities had no knowledge of the amount of actual residents who elected to stay in the city, and as a result, they were not fully prepared for what happened. Days of intense exposure to the sun's 95-degree smoldering heat and the lack of provisions resulted in an uninhabitable place of refuge. Conditions worsened so quickly that even the strongest man or woman could not withstand the pressures. Poor bathroom conditions and other problems developed as some waited for days to be rescued. In addition, at the Superdome and Center, rumors of riots, rape, and murder traveled throughout the city, state, and nation as fast as the gusting winds of the storm.

Like the spread of a disease, fear embraced the city, and rescue efforts were stifled early as crews feared being attacked by the confused evacuees of the Superdome and Convention Center. Mass chaos seeped throughout as looting and wild acts of violence brought lawlessness to a city once policed by a force respected by its residents. In some areas of the city and surrounding lower parishes, survivors began to cover rooftops like birds resting on their nests as homeowners broke out of their attics with axes while others swam to rooftops with the rising waters. Men, women, and children huddled closely while waiting to be rescued.

As survivors struggled, officials argued. Confusion between city, state, and federal authorities contributed to slow relief efforts, and some victims sat on their rooftops for hours upon days while confusion lead to desperation and desperation lead to despair. As the media bombarded the state, finger pointing and political rhetoric spread through the airways, and the helpless were left to fend for themselves while the agencies sought to repair damage.

Forgotten amongst the chaos of New Orleans, locals in St. Bernard and St. Tammany organized the rescue of their citizens. Relief workers from the Coast Guard, Wild Life and Fisheries and anybody with a flat boat assisted in the efforts in New Orleans while the limited forces of the NOPD and National Guards Men of Louisiana tried to control the masses in the dome, center, and streets.

With the downing of the towers of communication systems, all contact with area code residents of 504 and 985 were severed to the outside world. No one expected the destruction to close off all communications in the area. There was no contact with officials in St. Bernard, St. Tammany, and Jefferson, and fears for the worst entered as they took the brunt of the storm. The uncertainty lead to increased fear, and it seemed as if the wrath of nature finally turned Louisiana into a wasteland of hopelessness.

No one predicted that this would be the most destructive hurricane to hit the tri-state area of Louisiana, Mississippi, and Alabama since Betsy and Camille. Furthermore, no state could have prepared for any disaster, natural or terrorists attack, as unpredictable as this. Hours, days, and even years of preparation could not have prevented the problems that arose as each day ended, and no contingency plan could have foreseen the need for "what if" plans. All expert emergency preparedness plans floated down Canal Street with the flooding waters, and new plans were implemented on an event-by-event need.

As people throughout the world were pressed to their televisions for the first graphic images of the devastation, no one could have imagined or prepared for something that was as massive and destructive as this storm. Those first images shocked and terrified all as they watched the live suffering of many on television news agencies. With the rising of waters, flooding of homes, and increasing numbers of homeless, the stories of despair began to surface. These are the stories of the suffering survivors. Most are homeless, jobless, and separated from loved ones. If Katrina means pure, she was pure hell to most residents of Louisiana. Katrina, the purifier, will be labeled the storm of the century.

CHAPTER 3

The Shelter

As communities were uprooted, new ones were formed in the centralized confinement of the shelter. Each person was placed in his own sectioned community where families united and called their space, home. Rows and rows of makeshift bedding made from air mattresses to small cots were placed neatly in each section called the apartments by some. Numbers were assigned to these apartment sections to keep housekeeping duties flowing orderly. When certain numbers were called over the PA system, those groups or communities then proceeded to eat, bathe, or do whatever was required at that specified time. In this space, there was no privacy, but there was a sense that this is my home for now.

Home is a place where families unite and feel safe in the embracing arms of one another. For some, that hadn't been lost here in the shelter. However, the nucleus of the family enlarged, and each resident watched out for the other.

When a volunteer or new comer arrived at Lamar, his first vision was one of colorful masses of people. Black, White, Hispanic, Asian, rich, poor, middle class, educated, uneducated, criminal and non-criminal were all housed in an open area. Possessions were exposed and conversations were overheard, but still this was home.

This was the sentiment of many who were sheltered at Lamar Dixon Center in Gonzales. Most of the residents realized that their stay was not just for one night but for six months to a year. With this in mind, many prepared to enroll their children in schools and also to find employment. The difficult part of the day was the continuous boredom.

What follows here are the stories of those that survived the storm and are making new lives for themselves. They don't consider themselves refugees because they are residents and citizens of the United States of America, but they do consider themselves survivors.

In hopes of giving these survivors a venue for sharing their stories, I have documented from Lamar the stories of hope, horror, pain, and suffering. As you read this documentation, envision the lives of the survivors before, during, and after the storm. Their lives will forever be changed, and our country will forever be united in a cause to assist our own with a common bond of compassion and generosity through the goodness that was found in this darkness.

CHAPTER 4

The Forgotten

I had been to Lamar to drop off items needed for the survivors of the storm, but I had no idea that I would return to document stories of these survivors. When I arrived at Lamar, a friend, Rhonda Laiche introduced me to Mr. And Mrs. Ralph Perez. She had been assisting numerous evacuees with locating their missing loved ones. Under a tarp-covered tent, I sat at a table with the Perezes who began to share their story.

Ralph Perez is a retired long shore man out of New Orleans, and Barbara, his wife, is a faithful homemaker. On most days, Ralph went to the coffee shop where he drank coffee with his close friends while Barbara attended church, and it is her faith that has gotten her through this ordeal. Their community is comprised of Canary Island descendants where as Barbara says, "Everybody knows everybody, and we are all related and intermarried in some way."

Before the storm came to shore, Barbara and Ralph's son, who is handicapped, was evacuated to a nursing home in St. Francisville, Louisiana. Ralph and Barbara went to search for their son. They were housed in St. Franciseville Manor for one night but were evicted after spending the storm night there because a movie company booked the manor for three weeks. Then, they were moved to a local school which was an evacuation shelter. After a one-night stay at the school, once again they were evicted because the school was opening the next day. Fear and uncertainty engulfed them. The continuous rejection and eviction put much stress on the couple, and Ralph looked away as Barbara told me about it.

Their final destination and place of residence for the present time was here at Lamar where they seemed content and pleased with the hospitality of the locals.

After the storm, they didn't have any contact with family or friends because many of the 504 and 985 area codes were not working properly. Their only contact with family was through Rhonda who located family members and assured them that Ralph and Barbara were safe. They discovered that many of their family members were scattered in shelters throughout the country. Barbara's brother, who is serving in Iraq, was finally reassured that his family was safe but scattered.

After a few days, the phone systems began to work somewhat properly, and the Perezes contacted some of their neighbors who decided to ride the storm out. One neighbor was so severely affected by the storm, the quick raging waters, and its aftermath that he refused to speak of it. He said that he watched from his rooftop as the Perezes' home was sliced in half by a huge pecan tree. When the water came pouring in St. Bernard, it was a matter of minutes before many had time to climb into a boat or on to a roof top. They received news that many of their friends had drowned, and they were not sure if they even evacuated. A nursing home near their house was filled with thirty dead residents who were allegedly abandoned by their caretakers. This is presently under investigation.

When Ralph and Barbara departed from St. Bernard, they left with nothing, and they are returning to nothing. Barbara says she is not returning and that Ralph would have to find a new coffee shop and make new friends. She and Ralph are upset with the Army Corps of Engineers for digging a channel that they believe caused the parish to be severely affected by the floodwaters. Their hope is to start over in a new place close to where their son will receive proper care.

I asked them how their faith has carried them through this devastating time, and Barbara said they attended a service at Lamar and noticed that the priest celebrating the mass was Father Frank, a priest whom she had known from her community.

She said to the Lord, "Lord, you sure went a long way to get him (her husband) to church."

Through it all, she maintains her faith and is helping to sustain her husband through the unpredictable events in their lives.

CHAPTER 5

Broken Promises

While talking to the Perezes, another survivor, Mrs. Elizabeth walked up to get information from Rhonda. It was then I
noticed that a young teenaged black girl come up behind us with

a Ziploc bag of candy. She seemed intent on eating all that candy, and I laughed to myself. Being a youth minister and teacher at the local community college, I was drawn to her and told her that I was interested in hearing her story about the events of the storm. She seemed interested and a little surprised that I even spoke to her.

Because of the heat, we all decided that it would be best if we went into the shelter for the interviewing. Barbara and Ralph invited me into the shelter where they were housed in section 9. When I walked into the shelter, the wall-to-wall sections divide by numbers overwhelmed me. Some people were lying down resting while others were visiting or preparing for the day. Constant announcements were being projected over the PA system, and I found it a little distracting at first, but after a while, I didn't notice the noise.

Just beyond section 9 or apartment 9, about two feet over, there were a clinic and also a pharmacy for those who needed care. Doctors and nurses were busy caring for the sick. In fact, one patient was being examined in Barbara's bed, but she didn't seem to care. She pointed out to me that the volunteers had gotten her and her husband matching baby blue blankets since they were a couple. It seemed to sooth her to know that she and Ralph were all they had left connected to St. Bernard. They began speaking to Rhonda, and so I took that as my cue to interview Mrs. Elizabeth and Roxxane, the teenager.

As I gazed into the beautiful hazel eyes of Roxxane, I said to myself that this girl has been through many storms in her life that were not hurricanes. I noticed the scars on her hands and arms. She had such a beautiful smile when she did smile, and she seemed a little quiet at first. I was hoping that my years of ministering to youth would aid me in having her share her story.

At first, Roxxane sat there staring at me and listening to me talk. It seemed that my words were just floating in the air, and she didn't seem to absorb any of them. Something I said sparked her interest, and she began to share her story of brokenness.

Roxxane Fernandez has no mother. Her mother died, and I'm not sure when because Roxxane spoke in one word or one sentence replies. She was in the shelter with her Aunt or Aunt-T as she called her. She said she had a dad that she didn't know and was forbidden to know because her grandmother didn't like him. She lived with her grandparents but didn't seem to have a close relationship with them. Her relationships were short-term, and she wasn't too interested in getting close to anyone because of these severed relationships.

When I asked her how her typical day was before the storm, she became quiet and tears started to fill her eyes. As tears welled up in her eyes, I assured her it was okay if she didn't want to speak, and I asked her the question again. I held her hand and comforted her. Then she revealed that she had a fight with her sister. She began crying because she hadn't located her sister to tell her she was sorry, and she felt as if all of this was her fault. I assured her that she was forgiven for fighting with her and that if she and her sister were not united her on earth that they would one day be reunited in the kingdom of God. I told her that the Red Cross could assist her in locating her through the Internet. This seemed to comfort her.

During the storm, Roxxane and her family were housed in their home on 1904 Deslond in New Orleans or the 9th Ward area. As the storm moved further north, the water rose when the levee was breeched by a barge that broke through the levee system.

When water gushed through, wood framed houses floated from their addresses down to a new residential neighborhood. Trapped in their house with water rising, Roxxane and her family moved to a higher floor to avoid the flooding water. Uncertain of her demise, Roxxane became fearful as she sat and waited to be rescued. Hours went by and rescue workers loaded boats with anyone seeking to leave. Roxxane was brought to safety and eventually transported to Dutchtown High School in Prairieville and later transferred to Lamar with her family.

I asked her how the events of the storm affected her or changed her, and she looked at me in the eyes and shrugged her shoulders. The roughness of her life had hardened her, but soon softness overcame her when I asked her about school.

The Lamar community began to enroll students in the area high schools, hoping to give the youth routine and normalcy to their lives. Roxxane enrolled at St. Amant High or the school with the gator as she described it. I asked her how her first day was, and she became silent again. Then, she said something that really shocked me.

She apologized for what she was about to say and said, "In New Orleans, I go to a school that all blacks."

I said that I was aware of that. She continued to tell me that because of her lack of exposure to white students that when she arrived at the rural school filled with 75% whites that she feared them because she always made fun of white people and thought that they would do the same to her. As she sat in the classroom, she slumped in her seat, waiting for teasing to start, but to her surprise, she was welcomed and offered assistance from the very students she feared. She was surprised because her perception was inaccurate. She said that she felt bad for judging the students and that she didn't realize that she was prejudiced. I further pressed to see if she learned a lesson from this, and she said that her lesson was to not make fun of people because she really didn't realize how nice people could be.

Roxxane seemed content after our talk, and I pulled out a

candy bar I had gotten earlier and gave it to her. Then, I asked her what was the one thing that she desired. She was quiet and said that she liked gospel music and would love to be part of the choir that was starting at Lamar. I said you can do and be anything you want. Then, I promised her that I would return with gospel music and a CD player for her. Her eyes seemed to brighten, and she said she wished that when kids passed by her that they wouldn't ignore the music but that they would sit and listen.

Later, that day, the girl of broken dreams was sitting with her CD player playing her gospel music while others listened, and so one of her dreams was fulfilled.

Roxxane's future is uncertain, but her hope is to be reunited with her sister and nephew.

CHAPTER 6

Minister of Hope

During my conversation with Roxxane, Mrs. Elizabeth Danniel sat and listened and offered spiritual support as I interviewed Roxxane and assured her that God has a purpose for her. Mrs. Elizabeth is a licensed minister from Harvey in Jefferson Parish. Her faith in God is strengthened by her struggles and hardships in life.

Several months before the storm in April of 2005, her youngest son, Patrick, eighteen, was murdered by robbers. She was filled with love and hope as she spoke to me about him. Patrick was a wonderful young man, and his death was senseless, but his purpose in life was much greater. It wasn't until his funeral that she discovered just how anointed he was.

Everyday, as Patrick traveled to school, he greeted an elderly woman on the street, but the woman never returned his greeting. One morning, the elderly lady asked him why he bothered since most young people didn't care about people anyway. He said that he was different and that he went to church and loved everyone. This comment affected the elderly woman tremendously.

At Patrick's funeral, this very woman stood up and announced how he had influenced her life by showing her hope, and as result of his daily greetings, she returned to church. This incident strengthened Elizabeth's hope and faith in God's purpose for all. Years before, she also lost her daughter to ovarian cancer and was raising her grandchildren.

In August, a few weeks before the storm, Elizabeth's husband was diagnosed with liver cancer. On Sunday, Elizabeth was visiting her husband at Mercy Hospital in New Orleans when news came that the storm was definitely heading her way. Because of his severe condition, she didn't want to evacuate. After checking on her husband, she went to pick up her only surviving daughter and grandson and headed home to prepare for the storm. When she arrived home, she prepared things, collected enough food and water and prayed. Elizabeth felt like this was a time for prayer and preparation for the Holy Spirit to come in to direct her path.

That path would soon take a turn into the turmoil of the night. During the night, the wind and rain increased as the storm approached Jefferson Parish. Wind measuring up to 145 miles per hour stressed her house. Water began to pour in as the roof caved inward, and her grandson's window was blown out while the door was removed from its hinges by the strong driving wind. The rain poured continuously. Even though she was prepared to stay in the house, she felt the Holy Spirit directing her to leave, so she and her thirty-three year old daughter and fifteen year old grandson decided to depart, despite the driving forces of the wind and rain. Later, the Harvey Canal overflowed causing much flooding in Elizabeth's neighborhood. If she would have stayed, she would have been trapped in her home for days until rescue, or she would not have survived. Never in one moment did she doubt God's purpose for her leaving.

Traveling down the interstate system during the storm on Monday morning, Elizabeth had no idea of where the path of God was taking her, but she prayed. She trusted that God would protect and lead her to the right place. It was then on her radio that she heard about Lamar. When she got there, she realized that the Lord "planted her feet there" to minister to the young, needy, and hopeless who sought refuge in the shelter.

She said, "Lamar is filled with people from all nationalities that need hope."

She was the one to bring it to them.

After she arrived at Lamar, her daughter who was sick worsened. The clinic doctors at the shelter discovered that she was a severe diabetic and was hospitalized. If Elizabeth would have stayed home, her daughter would possibly have died. Mrs. Elizabeth once again felt that the Holy Spirit brought her here so that her daughter could receive the proper care.

While at Lamar, she tried to contact her husband, but her efforts were unsuccessful since she didn't have the resources to do so until the Lord put Rhonda Laiche in her path to assist her. Through the Internet, Rhonda discovered that he was evacuated to a Florida hospital where he was receiving care. Rhonda contacted Elizabeth's boss and arranged payment for her to go to Florida.

I asked Mrs. Elizabeth how her faith had saved her from despair.

She said, "To trust in the Lord for he will never leave or forsake us."

She felt blessed even though she lost everything. She knew that the Lord would provide for her, for if she did what He said, He would pour out a blessing. She wants all to trust in the Lord because He blessed her with so much help. She believes that the storm was allowed to happen to bring all races, nationalities, and religions together to unite us.

She continued, "Through this storm, there are opportunities from churches and citizens to give others something to look forward to-to start a new life."

Her final thought is, "No matter what you are going through, there is always hope."

I asked her how the storm affected her, and she said that it made her a better minister. Before the storm, she ministered to people in her church and on the streets, but she wasn't ministering enough. She felt that she was brought to Lamar to minister to others. She also realized how important family is and how we all have a purpose that leads us to different paths that affect others and us.

At present, Mrs. Elizabeth is still at the bedside of her ill husband, and I know that she continues to trust in the Lord and His will for her life. The Lord continues to send her helpers and so her trust in Him is strengthened.

CHAPTER 7

The Underdog

After talking with Mrs. Elizabeth, Rhonda tapped my shoulder and said she wanted me to meet Donald C. Thomas whom she referred to as her brother. As I turned to shake his hand, I noticed a huge smile and bright eyes. We spoke briefly, and for some odd reason, I mentioned to him that I was a three-time cancer survivor. When I said this, he connected soulfully with me and said, "You are the one I want to talk to cause you know what it means to be the underdog."

I had to leave the shelter early, and so my visit with Donald was short. However, he invited me to apartment number three to talk about a movie script he had written, but there was one condition, I had to knock before I entered. I felt a connection with him because I love to write, and I teach writing. There was definitely something special about Donald. A few days later, when I knocked on his door, I met his family and discovered just how special this underdog was.

Donald and Patricia live in the heart of the city off of Elysian Fields. He is a self-employed man of multiple talents. During the day, he managed his small contractor's business, and in the evenings, he wrote songs and movie scripts. Pat is a hard working mother, holding down two jobs at the casino and Forever 21. On most mornings, when Pat left for work, Donald brought the girls to school; then, he began his day with his contracting business, fixing rooftops and other repairs needed by his clients. Like most middle class hardworking parents, their days began early and ended late after tucking in the their daughters, Paris and India

A week before the storm, Donald and some young men produced a theme rap song for the New Orleans Hornets, the state professional basketball team. Donald wrote the lyrics.

The signing for the contract was supposed to be the week following the storm. Donald was excited because this was his first huge contract and exposure to the music industry outside of New Orleans. He was looking forward to signing the contract with great enthusiasm, but the storm's arrival hindered all his dreams for the moment.

He and Pat were also preparing to buy a new home, but they decided not to because they felt a little apprehensive about the deal. Their feeling proved to be accurate because they learned later that the very house they were to buy was flooded by water.

On Saturday, two days before the storm, Donald watched the news to determine if the storm was arriving east or west of New Orleans. The final destination of Katrina determined his destination. Certain that waiting to leave on Sunday was safe, Donald concluded that it would take twelve to fourteen hours to evacuate the city. After hearing from the local newscasters that the storm was definitely heading his way, Donald and Pat along with their girls made plans to leave the city with his father-in-law who had a place of refuge at a friend's home in St. Francisville.

Driving through pounding rains and increased winds while creeping in extremely slow traffic, Donald and his family finally arrived fourteen hours later in St. Francisville at the friend's home. A normal trip would have taken about two hours through typical traffic flow. However, the contra flow was so horrendous that it took most evacuees hours to reach their destinations. Authorities were not prepared for the massive exodus from New Orleans and surrounding parishes. This would prove defective in the evacuation plans because many were stranded on highways during the storm still seeking shelter.

Once they arrived, Donald learned that the home was full. His father-in-law was accepted, but Donald and his family along with three elderly people were rejected and turned away to seek shelter elsewhere. Extremely frustrated and disappointed, Donald sought shelter quickly since Katrina was approaching in a matter of hours. Feeling compassion for the rejected elderly, Donald and Pat took them under their care and set off in search of a shelter. They arrived at West Feliciana High School where they were fed, but Donald's family could not bring the family dog, YaYa, in the shelter, so they slept in their vehicle during the storm while the three elderly evacuees slept inside. With their girls crying and hot and mosquitoes biting, Pat was depressed and cried often while trying to be strong for the girls. The intensity of an unknown future and fear began to slip in as each hour slowly passed. That night needless to say Donald and Pat got little sleep while the wind rocked their vehicle.

After spending a restless night in their vehicle, the next morning, they were told that they had to leave the shelter because the school was opening the following day. Authorities directed them to another school some distance away in Denham Springs. After driving for hours, once they arrived there, they were again rejected because this school was opening the following day also.

Extremely exhausted and desperate, tethering on the edge of despair, they heard about a fourth place, Lamar where they finally found safety, showers, food, and kindness, a place of refuge. Temporary showers were set up in the horse stables for the evacuees. Pat was happy just to take a shower even if the conditions were not normal. This simple every day ritual that most take for granted brought Pat such sanity to the craziness of the events that led them there. Finally, Donald settled his family and his three elderly friends in apartment number three where he watched over them as a shepherd watches his flock.

Donald believed that the Lord led them to Lamar and that he would be here until the end of his ordeal. His children were then enrolled in a public school set up a Holy Rosary Catholic church where they feel safe. Donald volunteered at the shelter and watched over Pat's family and his three elderly evacuees.

I asked Pat and Donald how the storm and the events that led them to Lamar affected them as a family, father, mother, wife, and husband. Tears filling her eyes, Pat emotionally related that she really missed sitting in her home, cooking, and doing all the daily routines that she took for granted, and if she had the opportunity to regain them all, she would appreciate them more. She further added that she would hold on to everything and cherish all in her life.

Donald shared that if he were told that he would lose all contact with his family, he would not have believed it. The storm and the events have led him to appreciate his family and the small things in his life better. He felt that God was working the whole time and that the change in people is a great improvement.

"People seem to care more," he related.

Most nights in the shelter Donald slept very little because he was worried constantly about who was in the shelter, the sex offenders, thieves, murderers, and rapists.

He said, "I sleep with one eye open and one eye closed because the shelter is filled with people from all areas of life from the rich, middle class, poor, prostitutes, housewives, and thieves."

Like the shepherd in the field watching over his flock, Donald watched all under his care. He provided the three elderly evacuees with the comfort and assurance of a good shepherd.

It is Donald and Pat's hope to return to their normal life. Donald feels that the storm has given him an opportunity to help others and touch them. Before the storm, they didn't have everything they wanted, but they had everything that they needed. They hope that their girls will return to their magnet school and that his clients and Pat's jobs will all return to normal. The simple things most of us complain about are their richest rewards.

The underdog's experiences in life have strengthened him to become the father, provider, husband, and protector that he is today. Strong family values are what they believe have held them together. They plan to return to New Orleans and start over and to share their experiences with others so that they can see the value of family, morals, and good role models.

Donald is presently pursuing getting his movie script published. The title of the work is the Underdog. Like the underdog from the cartoons, Donald came to the rescue for many who were in despair. He is fighting FEMA for aid because his insurance company won't pay for damage to his home, claiming that his flood insurance policy doesn't cover the loss. For others, benefits weren't honored because they didn't have flood insurance. The policies are confusing to many; either they have one policy or other, but they don't have coverage for either when the time comes for the insurance companies to reimburse the clients for damages. It seems that the insurance companies are like the tax collectors of Jesus' day. They take the people's money and exploit them. Donald, the underdog, will prevail through this trial too.

CHAPTER 8

100% U.S. Army – Truth

As I drove up to interview Chad Lynch, I noticed on his mail box US *Army* in bold lettering. I knew that this was a man who pledged to serve and protect his country no matter what the mission or sacrifice.

Two days before the storm hit, eighteen year veteran, First Sergeant Chad Lynch and the Louisiana National Guard, Charlie Company 769th Engineer Battalion, were deployed to Jackson Barracks located in the 9th Ward of New Orleans on the east end of the Mississippi river. Their mission was to assist the NOPD with rescue and recovery using their high water vehicles or troop carriers. These vehicles are high enough to go through floodwaters.

The first mission was to develop teams that would be dispatched with the New Orleans Police Department Officers (NOPD) throughout the districts of New Orleans. The captain of the NOPD and Chad's men paired up and departed from Jackson Barracks to view the districts and drop off the officers' police cars at the Hilton. Some police and troops were stationed that night in the districts or at the Hilton. The next morning the teams began their high water mission, but Chad and 15% of his troops were trapped in Jackson Barracks as water rose quickly to high levels in one hour.

As the storm blew through New Orleans with high winds, a barge rammed through the levee not far from the barracks. Predicting that the water might rise, earlier that night, Chad and his men prepared by bringing vital supplies and cots up to the upper levels of the barracks. Each man made two or three trips to the upper levels. By the time the men were on their last trip, the water had already risen to about mid chest. Water rose as high as eight to ten feet from ground level. The troops secured the third floor and hunkered down for the duration of the storm. With minimal generator power, there was very little lighting. As water rose quickly, some began to communicate with the National Guard chain of command for rescue.

It wasn't until the next morning that the two hundred men and women trapped in high water in the Barracks could assess the damage. With little to do but wait for rescue, some peered out of the garage door. They assessed that houses were moved from their very yards as water rushed in and uplifted them. Shingles were removed from some rooftops, and trees and vehicles were scattered along the street like toys in a tub of water. Some of the city's buses that arrived the day before to evacuate people were covered with water, and no floating bodies were visible to the peering troops.

After constant communications, a day and half later, the troops in the Barracks were finally rescued by boats on Tuesday night. A few hours later, they were finally evacuated from the barracks to the levee. Once they were safely placed at the levee, Black Hawk helicopters flew the troops to the Superdome. From this point on, the troops were in full force action, and their mission was redefined.

With lack of sleep and rest for many, days and nights became puzzling. The troops bunkered on the fifth floor of the dome while civilians occupied the first, second, and third floors.

Not hearing from the rest of his battalion, Chad tried to locate them. He discovered that the others along with the NOPD were already implementing the mission of search and rescue with the high water vehicles. However, the remaining force's mission at the dome changed form one of search and rescue to one of feed the need. Chad received information that assistance was needed at the docks, so the troops immediately departed. As needs of the people arose, new missions were implemented. Food and supplies were arriving at the docks, so the troops assisted in bringing the supplies to the dome for the civilians. In addition, a triage was set up at the dock as rescued survivors began to arrive. Minute by minute contingency plans were put in place for each changing role of the troops.

The Louisiana National Guard's Charlie Company 769th Engineer Battalion was divided into those assisting in high-water rescues and those assisting with distribution of food to the dome. Those at the dome were too valuable to leave it.

Numerous special force guards were policing the dome day and night. Many guardsmen were disbursed throughout the dome trying to keep the order of 25,000 evacuees. They fed people three meals a day while trying to keep order. Families were fearful and stressed, and rumors began to surface about rapes and murders of young women and children. However, none of this was factual. Chad related that while he was on guard one woman passing complained that the guards weren't doing their jobs. Concerned, Chad asked the woman to take him to the sight; however, once they arrived at the restroom, she confessed that she heard the rumor but couldn't prove to him that it was factual.

Chad spoke to a policeman in the area who proceeded to search the bathrooms, but he found no proof of such activity. At the dock where Chad's crew was assisting in the food distribution, there was a makeshift morgue where bodies where placed in a freezer. Chad observed that there were only three body bags there which did not come from the inside of the dome. It is his belief that none of these were of children or women who were raped and murdered in the dome. The rumors spread by a few stressed evacuees were aired throughout the country and world by reporters who did little investigation. This inadequate reporting hindered the efforts of those trying to maintain order within the dome, and high levels of anxiety filled the dome as these rumors became truth to some. Chad and another guardsman mingled with the people and concluded that even though immeasurable levels of anxiety existed the people were still orderly as long as their immediate needs of food and water were met. Chad felt that if these needs were not met then maybe chaos would result.

There was a moment of concern when the electricity provided by the generator threatened to fail. The generator was located in a room in the lower area of the dome consumed by water. Concerned about the diminishing fuel levels of the generator, the engineers of the guard developed a plan to refuel it without losing power to the dome. After much tribulation, they rigged a direct line from the fuel tank to the generator. Successful in their endeavor, the guard never lost electricity. As long as it was provided, the people maintained order within the dome. However, if they would have lost power, then possibly the rumors would have become truth, but the visible forces of the military prevented any of this from surfacing.

On the same night of the generator mission, there was an incident with a guardsman and a civilian. The civilian took the guardsman's gun as he tried to break up a fight and shot the guard in the leg. Then, later that night, after feeding the people, the guardsmen walked into the dome where a couch was set on fire. Smoke filled the dome, and fear that the dome was on fire spread quickly. However, that fear was doused as the guardsmen immediately removed a burning couch and secured the area. With the threats of losing electricity, the injured guardsman, and the burnt couch, levels of stress and fear increased.

I asked Chad about the Convention Center since he was so near it. At first, there was hardly anyone there he said. However, as the water rose, he noticed that people began to come from all parts of the city to the Convention Center. No one knew just how many people had stayed in New Orleans until they all started to wade their way to the center. The guardsmen were already stressed at the dome with 25,000 evacuees, and little forces were stationed at the center. Chad was concerned about the incoming people and consulted with a volunteer named Ray from FEMA who seemed to be maintaining people for the time being. It was then that Ray and Chad organized a mission to get food to these people. A couple of trucks dropped off food there for the small amount of people who started to arrive.

The feeding operations at the dome were more of a concern since the numbers of evacuees were higher. Organized efforts were made to feed the 25,000 at the in-zone of the dome. Chad said it was like Mardi Gras; the mass of people was so great that they had to throw Meals Ready To Eat (MRE's) to the crowd to get food to them. As buses began to arrive, the operations of the Charlie Company shifted from one of feed the need to one of securing the buses as continuous lines of evacuees extended around the dome.

School districts from all areas of the state offered their buses for the evacuation of the dome. However, as the media began to spread rumors of mass chaos at the dome, the bus operations were halted by the districts out of fear that the bus drivers would be compromised. After the districts were assured that the bus drivers would be safe, the evacuation plans were reinstated. Long lines and hot weather strained the people, and the guard had to preserve order in the lines. Because they feared losing their spot in line, some people stood in line as long as a day and a half, and some did faint from lack of water and extreme heat. Once the area was secured, the evacuation of the dome moved more smoothly, and the people began to see rays of hope and thanked the guards for their efforts.

A team from Oklahoma arrived and relieved the guardsmen who were then moved to another mission. Finally, with the mission of the dome sealed, the 769th's mission shifted to an engineering mission. After the regrouping of the battalion, the 769th moved to their mission of clearing the streets. They began to clear trees, cars, and debris to make way for rescue. They were ordered to not retrieve any bodies from the streets because of biohazards and their lack of training to handle the bodies, but they were to make note by calling in information so that later the appropriate teams could retrieve the bodies. Some of the dead were tagged by loved ones and placed along the side of the streets.

The 769th cleared many streets of rubble. Rumors of gang activity didn't hinder their mission. In the early days of the storm, the high-water rescue team encountered gun shots, but the soldiers couldn't defend themselves because at that time they were not equipped with weapons, but after this while clearing the streets, in order to protect themselves, the guardsmen were issued weapons.

In the 9th ward area, the houses were devastated as the raging waters totally wiped out whole blocks of communities. Where once children jumped rope and played games, only slabs remained. Oil from a Petrochemical company, mixed with water, contaminated the streets and homes. The homes and area were uninhabitable; the sewer system mingled with the water and filled the area with biohazard materials.

While clearing the area, the 769th saw much affliction in the faces of people they encountered who chose to stay in their homes. While clearing the streets, eleven days after the storm, they encountered a rescue unit from El Paso, Texas who asked them to take the high water truck into Desire where they heard of two people who needed to be rescued. A woman in her forties stood on her porch waving to get their attention. Ms. Ross had been in her home with her mother who had been dead for five days. They picked her up and marked the house for body recovery. They brought her to an ambulance. The woman had been using dirty dish water to wash her dishes and drinking the contaminated water. She was dehydrated, hungry, and severely stressed by the days she spent with her deceased mother.

I asked Chad if he had any concerns during the whole operation. His only concerned was for his three daughters and his wife Jeanie because he had heard rumors of disturbance at a shelter in his community not far from his residence. Knowing that there were rapists and child molesters in the shelter, he expressed concern for the safety of his family, but his fears were dispelled after he communicated with local police and confirmed that like the dome these too were just rumors.

In addition to this, he expressed that the finger pointing was not necessary since those pointing the finger were not involved in the operations of the city and had no idea of the complications of the operations. Before the storm, the NOPD and the National Guardsmen were set in place, but no one predicted that the levee system would fail. No community could have been prepared. The number of people remaining in the city caused a challenge, but each challenge was met with a plan, and the problems were eventually conquered by the dedication of the troops.

I asked Chad if there was any other incident that affected him, and he said that he noticed after the buses had evacuated, there was a dog abandoned and tied to the door knob of the dome. Thinking of his family, he brought the dog home to them and named her Katrina.

Chad's final mission is to let the truth be known. It is through this venue that he is doing this. Morale of the troops was never low, and the New Orleans policemen were faithful to their mission despite the few who abandoned their pledge to serve and protect. He continued that the people of the dome are just like any of us. Put in a stressful situation, people overreact, but once these people were placed on a bus, their hope returned, and they thanked the guardsmen for protecting them.

Lesson learned: rumors spread by the media created havoc. The rumors were never investigated by sources whose responsibility was to report to the public the absolute truth, and so a city and state are scared by the media's lack of professionalism.

CHAPTER 9

Hurricane Watch

Ashley Simoneaux is a CT Technologist who lives in Metairie and works at Tulane Medical Center. I first heard about her story from her parents who hadn't heard from her two days after the storm.

Two days before the storm, Ashley was in Baton Rouge preparing to shop for furniture in Alexandria, Louisiana when she received a page from the hospital requesting that she return to the city because someone on hurricane watch didn't return. She wasn't scheduled for hurricane watch since she was on the previous watch, but because one of the employees evacuated, she was called into work. After collecting a few personal items from her apartment in Metairie, she returned to Tulane with very little possessions and money. Ashley along with another employee decided to stay on watch. When others started to arrive and assist, she decided to return to her apartment to collect her dog, Rigley, and a few items. Not certain of the length of her stay, she only brought enough food and items for four days. She made plans to have her dog evacuated to Houston, but he was not taken, so she had to sneak him into the hospital through the back doors. Others did the same with their animals.

The administrators told her that they would be locked in the hospital for at least four days. Many nurses, doctors, and staff prepared for a short stay and not longer. They spent the night in the hospital, and weathered the storm well, but the next morning as the levee system burst, all changed quickly. Electricity was lost, but the generators kept the red plugs running and necessary power to keep patients on vital machinery. The staff, nurses, doctors, patients, and their families went to the center of the building where there were no windows to view the actions on the outside. With the flash lights, refrigerator and cells plugged in, they felt that they would be comfortable for a while. However, they didn't predict that events outside would prevent their rescue.

By the third day, about fifty people from the streets tried to break into Tulane. Frightened for the patients, the hospital personnel locked the emergency room doors and put a security guard on watch. The police officers ordered the hospital employees to remain in the hospital and not venture out because they were concerned for their safety. At one point, there were some drug users pounding on the doors trying to break in through the emergency room. Fearful, the staff moved back and focused on getting the patients out of the hospital.

After communicating with The Hospital Corporation of

America or HCA, the employees were assured that helicopters provided by the agency would arrive to rescue only the patients. Slowly the patients were evacuated, but as water began to rise, the elevators that they were using shut down and patients had to be hoisted from the seventh floor down to the evacuation level. They put the patients on mattresses and sliding boards and slid them down seven flights of stairs. One patient weighed 430 lbs. With patience and persistence, he was taken to the garage roof and evacuated with the others. Patients were placed in the helicopters. Some were so disabled that they had to be loaded in wheel chairs onto the helicopters.

After the patients were evacuated, on the third day, the families of the patients were rescued by boat. HCA didn't provide the means for the families' evacuation. The Wild Life and Fisheries crews took hours to evacuate all the families. They promised the staff that they would return to remove them, but because of the firing from the snipers and gangs, the efforts of the Wild Life and Fisheries were halted until the area surrounding the hospital was secured.

Anxious and nervous, the staff by the fourth day began to wonder if they would ever be rescued. Food was scare since the employees sacrificed their rations and gave most of it to the patients and neglected themselves. They began to rummage through the vending machines where they appeased their hunger with sugar filled items like Rice Crispy Treats in addition to tuna.

They were ordered by rescue workers to not return to the ground floor because the helicopters were being fired upon while trying to evacuate, so they moved to the second floor, hoping that this would be their place of rescue. However, nothing transpired, and they were then ordered to move to the third floor. Each time they were moved, they left precious food and water behind since they couldn't haul it all from floor to floor. With several hundred staff, nurses, and doctors along with their animals still trapped, the rescue efforts were once again called off. Sounds of gun fire were heard, and by this time, many began to worry if they would ever be rescued. With no electricity and bathroom facilities, they had to use whatever means they could.

On the fifth day, once again the police ordered them to move to the seventh floor. When they reached the fifth floor, they heard gun fire and hunkered down there. Abandoning their provisions, they had to drink out of the same bowls as the animals and had to use kitty liter and red bags for a bathroom. Their provisions were low. Four boxes of Pop Tarts and two gallons of water were all that were left. Waiting for rescue was not easy as stomachs growled and the discussion to put the animals to sleep was debated. Frustration was high, and each time they were moved and promised rescued, their hopes were chipped away. Finally, later on the fifth day, with the area being secured, the Black Hawk helicopters were able to move to the roof top of the garage. Ashley, her dog, and others boarded the helicopters.

After boarding the Black Hawk, they arrived at the New Orleans airport where they remained for six hours before being bused to Lafayette, Louisiana. The buses were provided by HCA. Once they arrived in Lafayette, they were not allowed to leave the buses because authorities feared they were contaminated. Not having a bath for five days, they only desired to get off the bus and clean themselves. Three national guardsmen with guns prevented them from exiting the bus. After decontamination, Ashley and her dog, Rigley, were finally safe. After five days of being trapped in Tulane, Ashley finally returned to her parents' home where she is for now until she decides what her future will be.

With Ashley's future uncertain, she contemplates returning

to Tulane. She loved her job, and the people she worked with, but the water damage to Tulane was so tremendous that she doesn't know if she will return. She said what she has learned from the whole incident is to be more patient, and she has realized that she is a stronger person now that she has suffered through this ordeal.

During her suffering in Tulane her boyfriend, a Jefferson Parish police officer, tried to rescue her. Her night and shining armor was unsuccessful as he was fired upon too by gang members. Little communication between Ashley and her family stressed them, but by the grace of God, they were able to establish contact for some strange reason for only a short moment to assure them that she was safe and awaiting rescue.

Ashley's advice to all is for all to appreciate what they have and to not complain about the littlest things. Patience is a great virtue. She has gained that through her suffering. Ashley's experience with hurricane watch will be one she will always remember. No training could ever prepare anyone for the unknown.

CHAPTER 10

The Aftermath

Four weeks after Katrina, many residents of New Orleans and surrounding parishes were still housed in shelters seeking apartments, trailers, and rental property. FEMA provided some funds for housing but only for three months. With no jobs or pay checks coming in, most wonder if they will ever rise up out of this desolate situation in their lives. Many seek counseling as they begin to come to terms with their ordeals.

During their time of recovery, another storm, Hurricane Rita, threatened the Louisiana coastal region, but this time she missed New Orleans and the southeastern portion of the state. Like Katrina, Rita a category four, destroyed much of the coastal cities in the western half of the state. Lake Charles, Ester, and many other communities received extensive damage from high water and strong winds. Rebuilding for them is just beginning. Loss of lives was minute since the lessons of Katrina prompted people to evacuate early. However, the same traffic jams and slow moving evacuations occurred.

As Katrina's victims identify with the loss of Rita's survivors, they prepare to return home to assess the damages. Houses in St. Bernard, Venice, Chalmette and other lower lying areas were totally wiped out by flood waters. Rebuilding seems futile. Hopes are faded as each day brings news of losses.

New Orleans residents faired a little better. Their levees were repaired, but the problems still exist. This was evident when Rita arrived, and uninterrupted rainfall stressed the levees while water once again flooded the 9th Ward. Some say this was a blessing because all the contaminated area would be washed clean by the fresh water. As some returned to their homes, their hopes were high as they saw the structures still standing, but when they entered their homes, grief filled their hearts as they realized that the high water caused widespread damage. All is lost.

As these citizens prepare to rebuild their lives, they are bombarded with new struggles with insurance companies. Companies refuse to provide for the long term policy holders because their policies don't include flood insurance. This was a disaster, and they should pay some argue. New definitions will have to be formed as questions arise as to what is considered covered under their policies.

While the citizens fight this battle, the state and local agencies contend with the finger pointing of the federal agencies. Committees are formed to investigate and evaluate what went wrong. FEMA'S director, Michael Brown, is relieved of his duties as a result of the negative reports of his handling of the disaster. Politicians debate with FEMA's Michael Brown on his agency's role in the disaster. For those involved, the police officers, military, volunteers, and state agencies, no plan could have prepared any state for the natural disaster of Katrina. The issue should not be what went wrong, but how can we fix it? As Texas saw, one main problem is with the traffic jams. How can the states better prepare their citizens in times of disaster? Another concern should be for the improvement of the levee system. For years, many political leaders of the state have tried to appropriate funds from the federal government to improve the system, but the immediate need was not measured correctly, and as a result, the unimaginable occurred. These are the issues the federal, state, and local politicians need to tackle. If this were an attack by terrorists, with no warning, no plan could have averted the problems that arose as minute by minute, hour by hour, new missions were implemented and new situations developed.

The suffering survivors of Katrina continue to endure the pain of their losses as they try to rebuild a new future for themselves and families. Countless stories of survival are surfacing. Many are beginning to share their experiences as they seek counseling. When some hear what others have suffered, they realize that their blessings are many.

One such story was of a young boy who was sitting on his rooftop with his family. As he was being lifted up to the helicopter, he was dropped several feet into the water. Since the incident, he has never been the same. His parents hold him tightly each night and are afraid to let him out of their sight.

Another story is of a man who lived in St. Bernard. At ten that morning, he thought that the storm had finished, but he received a call from his neighbor who saw water rushing into town. The man looked out of his door and saw the water rolling toward his house. He called to his wife to get her into a boat, but she was too concerned about the dog and froze after she saw the water rushing towards them. In a matter of minutes, the water consumed the house, and the husband searched for hours for his wife in the high water until rescue workers retrieved him from the water and promised to bring him to look for his wife. Weeks later, his wife's body was found still in the house.

Numerous experiences such as these are familiar to many. Years of therapy will never repair all the material or mental damage done. With Rita's arrival, the focus now turns to the labors of the southwestern part of the state.

As these super storms continue to hammer the coastal states, innovative procedures are needed to better prepare citizens for evacuation out of the danger zone. Insurance companies must better define their policies to their clients so that the customers can best maximize their coverage. Governmental agencies should implement an outline of preparedness for all disasters, natural or unnatural. Finally, the news agencies have to stop exaggerating tragedies for their economical gain and high ratings. Many rescue efforts were blocked because of the vicious rumors spread by the panic of a few to the voracious reporters.

Katrina's impact on the state and nation will forever be a constant reminder of the astronomical devastation of a state and her citizens. The road of recovery will be winding and lengthy, but many vow to return to their homes and rebuild their lives.

Katrina, the purifier, has united the state and its citizens. Through adversity, many have reached out to others they may not have otherwise helped in a different situation. Barriers were blown down as the charity of many extended beyond their normal means. A nation built on unity will survive the most difficult situations, for it is through adversity that we are strengthened.

CHAPTER 11

New Horizons: Starting Over

As the sun is rising over the state of Louisiana, the survivors awaken from their shelters and new rental homes. After assessing their losses, some realize that it will be months and years before they recover from the demolition of their lives. However, there is hope.

Those that I interviewed have taken paths in their lives that they never thought they would venture, and some who vowed to never return grasp that home is where they lived most of their lives and that community is important as well as family. As a result of this revelation, they prepare to return, maybe not now, but later.

The Perezes have returned to their daughter's home, which was filled with water, but still useable. They reconnected with their long time friends and buried those that didn't survive.

Roxanne continues to attend school, but her attitude towards others has worsened. She disrupts the class and is unfriendly, and many of the students who tried to reach out to her have given up. With her hope destroyed, she has little to look forward to as each day she returns to the cold metal building called home.

Mrs. Elizabeth has returned from Florida with only her husband's ashes. His purpose in life was not to survive the cancer. Because she couldn't afford to fly his body home, she had to have his body cremated so that she could have a proper service for him with his family. Through it all, the people of Florida have opened their arms to her and helped her. She continues to stay in touch with Rhonda. For now, this minister of faith lives with her son who married his long time girlfriend during the storm in Denham Springs, but she searches for her new place to call home, knowing that a new beginning for this couple will demand no mother-in-law.

After forty days and nights in the shelter, Donald C. Thomas and his family have moved into a rental trailer, purchased a truck, and established home in an unfamiliar surrounding to this life time city dweller in the rural community of St. Amant, Louisiana, my hometown. The community has opened its arms to this family, and they learn how the rural residents operate.

No water bills here. Donald and Pat were surprised that most of the water comes from underground wells that pump water to the home. They thought when they were told this that they would have to actually go to an above ground well and hoist a bucket up to get water. To their relief, this is not so. Donald likened his experience to the <u>Green Acres</u> sitcom. He has had to learn to drive a little faster in the country and not thirty-five miles per hour like in the city. In addition, gun fire heard in the early morning and late evening is the sound of hunters looking for rabbits or squirrels during the opening season. Through it all, he has maintained a sense of humor where most men would have broken after living openly in a shelter for forty long days and nights.

His neighbors in the all white neighborhood have embraced him and his family and have offered many items to replace the ones they lost in their home that was filled to the ceiling with contaminated water.

Pat lost all her pictures of her children and wedding day, but she has the real thing. The every day items that cannot be replaced are gone forever, but her new hope is to make new albums of her family. Tasks that didn't seem so important to her are now valuable. A long hot bubbly bath is heavenly, and cooking a home cooked meal is no longer a chore. Donald and Pat realize that their stay is long term.

First Sergeant Chad Lynch continues his mission weeks after the storms, Katrina and Rita. He has been promoted to Sergeant Major and visits his family every chance he gets.

Ashley is working in Baton Rouge and is determining whether she will return to New Orleans or not. She appreciates the little times she has with her parents and Rigley, her dog.

Life as these people have known has changed forever, but their suffering through Katrina has made them resilient. Their faith and family are most important. No storm can take that from them, for it is through suffering that we are purified.

CHAPTER 12

Reflection

After speaking with these victims, it becomes clear that many have suffered losses that can never be measured in material value. The children left behind their homes, neighborhoods, friends, and schools. Senior years were destroyed. Graduations with lifetime friends washed away with the waters of the lake and river. Proms, football games, championships, and many other teen events were all destroyed by wind and rain in one day. This year will be one that many will remember for a lifetime. No stories of a great senior year will be written in diaries or journals.

This sense of loss for the youth was apparent to me as I walked through the campus of a school established at my church for the children of the shelter. Some eight graders were sitting in the courtyard of the church with their teacher. No sounds of laughter or conversations came from the group. The teacher tried to encourage them, but it seemed to me these were a generation of children broken by the losses of their young lives. Years of therapy cannot remove the pain embedded deep within their youthful hearts.

Not only are the civilians or residents victims but also the police force. Multiple stories with similar endings filled the state. Accounts of NOPD officers committing suicide surfaced. While attending to the city's needs, many of these officers left their families not knowing just how badly things would get and returned home to find loved ones deceased. In utter despair, some took their lives. The sacrifice of these men cost them their families and lives.

However, the storm did spew many unsung heroes among the nurses, doctors, police, and military forces. What these people experienced through their professions will forever mark them and change them. Without ceasing, they continued their duties with little sleep or food for themselves. Fear crippled their efforts but never did they lose sight of their missions. The very people who were trained to assist others in disastrous situations never predicted that they too would need to be rescued.

Not only did the children suffer, but also the adults who had so much already invested in their lives. They lost jobs, security, homes, and their sanity. These times reminded me of the novel, *The Grapes of Wrath*. Many of the potato farmers in this novel were displaced living in makeshift shanties, poor, confused, and hungry for something better, and in Louisiana, there are a number of displaced residents disbursed throughout the nation living in shelters seeking better. Adults looking to provide for their families are helpless. Without jobs and funds, they are totally reliant upon the kindness of their neighboring parishes, states, and government. Some never thought they would have to hold a hand out for assistance, but many swallowing pride had to since all was lost. Some because of their resilience will survive, and others will rupture under the pressures of despair.

WORKS CITED

Cover Photo of Donald's home. Personal photograph by Donald C. Thomas. 6 Oct. 2005.

Danniel, Elizabeth. Gonzales. Personal photograph by author. 10 Sept. 2005.

Danniel, Elizabeth. Personal interview. 10 Sept. 2005.

Fernandez, Roxanne. Gonzales. Personal photograph by author. 10 Sept. 2005.

Fernandez, Roxanne. Personal interview. 10 Sept. 2005.

Gyan, Joe and Millhollon, Michelle.. "Levees fail: N.O. Submerged." The Advocate 31 Sept. 2005 http://2theadvocate.com/soties/083105/new_levees0001.shtml.

Lynch, Chad. St. Amant. Personal photograph by author. 22 Sept. 2005.

Lynch, Chad. Personal interview. 22 Sept. 2005.

Perez, Barbara. Gonzales. Personal photograph by author. 10 Sept. 2005.

Perez, Ralph. Gonzales. Personal photograph by author. 10 Sept. 2005

Perez, Barbara. Personal interview. 10 Sept. 2005.

Perez, Ralph. Personal interview. 10 Sept. 2005.

Shelter Picture. Gonzales. Personal Photograph by author. 22 Sept. 2005.

Simoneaux, Ashley. Prairieville. Personal photograph by author. 26 Sept. 2005.

Simoneaux, Ashley. Personal interview. 26 Sept. 2005.

Thomas, Donald C. Gonzales. Personal photograph by author. 22 Sept. 2005.

Thomas, Patricia. Gonzales. Personal photograph by author. 22 Sept. 2005.

Thomas, Donald C. Personal interview. 22 Sept. 2005.

Thomas, Patricia. Personal interview. 22 Sept. 2005.

362271

Made in the USA